The RescueLogic® Announcer Guide

How to Add Audible Emergency Alerts to your RescueLogic System

Cadgraphics Incorporated
Makers of RescueLogic Software for Fire and Security Systems

"Safety Made Simple"

PO Box 11737
St. Paul, MN 55111-0737

Website: www.rescuelogic.com
Email: info@rescuelogic.com
Phone: (612) 722-3233

ISBN 978-0692244296

June 2014

Table of Contents

A Note about Illustrations

This guide is illustrated with actual RescueLogic screen images, which were captured on a computer that runs Windows 7. If your computer uses a different Windows operating system, your RescueLogic windows might look different, but you will follow the same step-by-step procedures.

Introduction: The RescueLogic Announcer Program

RescueLogic's Announcer is an add-on program that plays audible emergency alerts when the devices in your RescueLogic system go into trouble or alarm. With Announcer, it's easy to customize your own emergency messages, so everyone knows what's going on.

Things You'll Need:

To get the most from RescueLogic's Announcer program, you will need:

- RescueLogic software with a licensed copy of the Announcer module.
- A text-to-speech program. We recommend NaturalReader's professional version, which makes it possible to create and save sound files.

Additional Requirements for Public Address Systems:

If you're going to broadcast audible alerts over a public address system, you will also need:

- A relay switch that will control signals from Announcer to your sound system, which will act like the "press to talk" button on a microphone. Announcer is designed to work with Advantech's ADAM-6060 module, available online or from industrial control suppliers.
- Network information. You'll need to get a static IP address from your network administrator wherever a serial server is to be installed. For each serial server, the network administrator should also provide values for the Subnet Mask, Default Gateway, and possibly DNS Servers.
- Audio cables to connect the audio output on your computer to your site's sound system.
- You'll need to ensure that the audio output of your computer has enough power to be compatible with the amplifier of your sound system. You may need to purchase a pre-amp device to boost the signal.

Overview

The Announcer program generates audible alerts based on the device types in your system, along with their locations and conditions. Each audible announcement will describe an alarm, broadcast its location, and transmit emergency "Take Action" instructions.

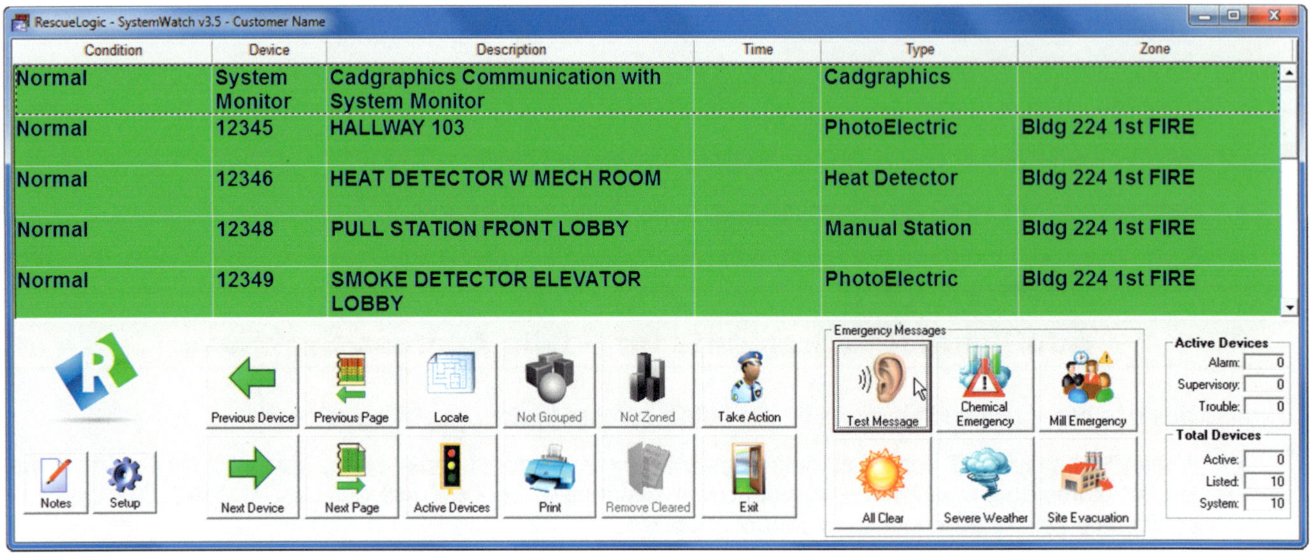

Helpful Hint: You will need to install RescueLogic's main program before you can install the Announcer feature.

Technical Background

Here's how the Announcer program works.

A basic RescueLogic system consists of three programs:

1. **Configuration Manager**, which administrators use to set up and configure each RescueLogic system.
2. **System Monitor**, which receives and sorts data from the alarms and panels on your site. In the process, System Monitor segments alarm information into categories
3. **System Watch**, which displays that data in the form of color-coded lists, maps, floor plans, and action messages.

The Announcer program gets segmented data from System Monitor, too. Announcer combines that data with sound files. Those sound files correspond to the eight categories that constitute a RescueLogic "Take Action" message: prefix, panel, type, device, location, zone, group, and suffix.

The result is a seamless audible announcement that you can hear from your computer or broadcast on a public-address system.

Step 1: Install the Announcer Program

Announcer is an optional component designed to enhance your RescueLogic system. You might have received a download link for a trial version of RescueLogic, or you might have already licensed the software package. In either case, you should have RescueLogic installation files on your computer.

If you followed our download instructions, the download files are in a folder called “RescueLogic Install,” and you'll find it on drive C.

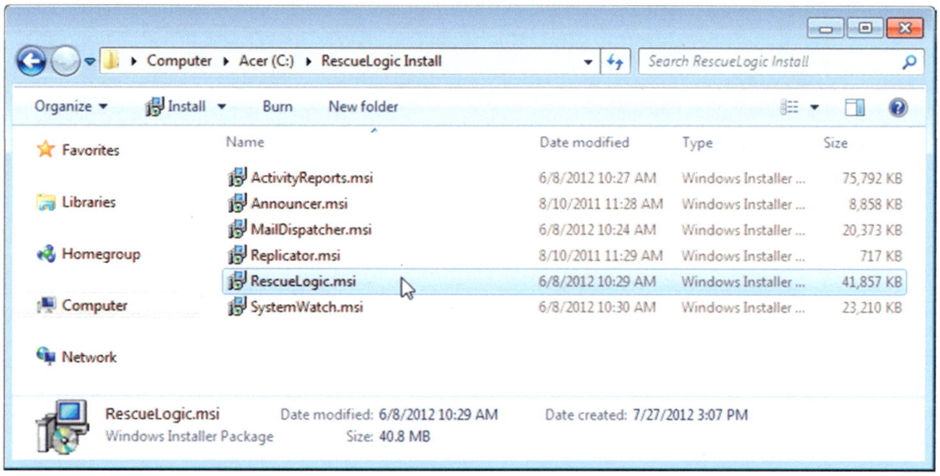

Double-click on “Announcer.msi” to open and install the program. (If you can't find it, search for “Announcer.msi.”)

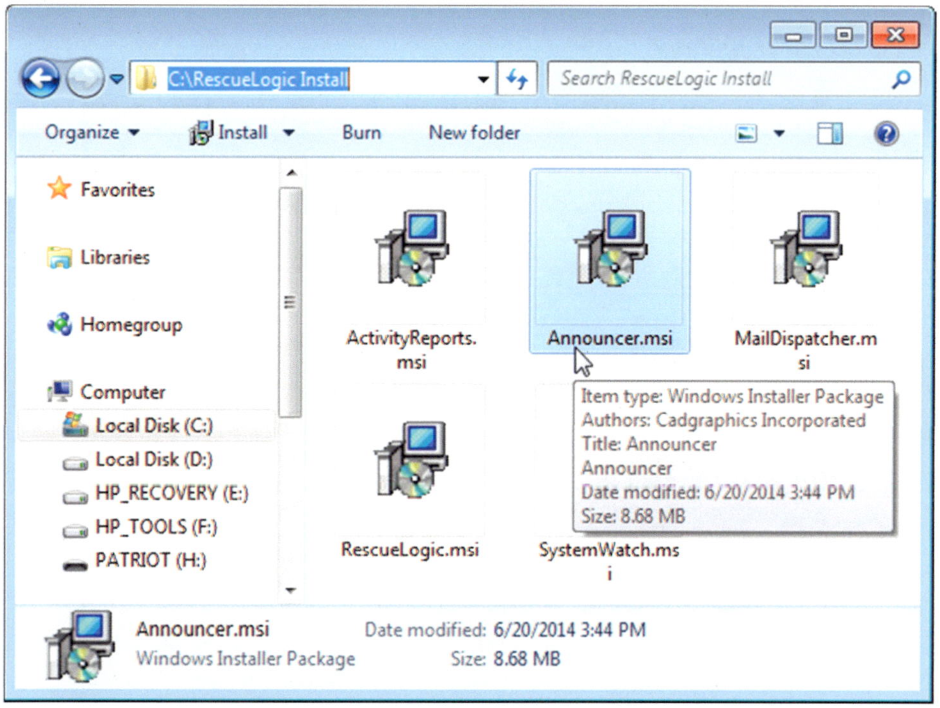

Helpful Hint: One way to open a folder on your hard drive or on another computer is to type the folder name as a command. Click the “Start” button, and then click Run. Now type the program name.

The Setup Wizard

The Setup Wizard will open. Click “Next” to continue.

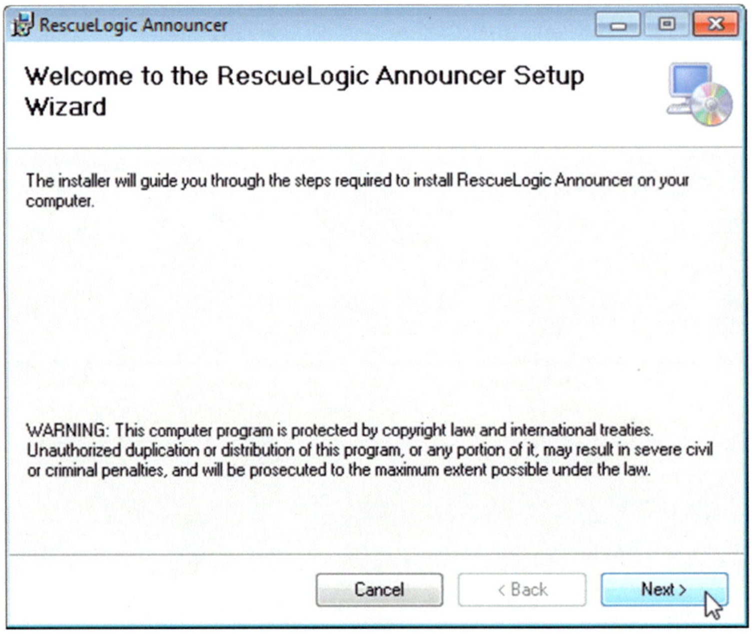

License Agreement

Read and accept the license agreement.

Install Announcer

Click “Next” to install Announcer in the default folder on drive C, or “Browse” to install it in a different location. (Please note that you must install Announcer in the same folder as the main RescueLogic database. If you follow standard setup instructions, it will go there automatically.)

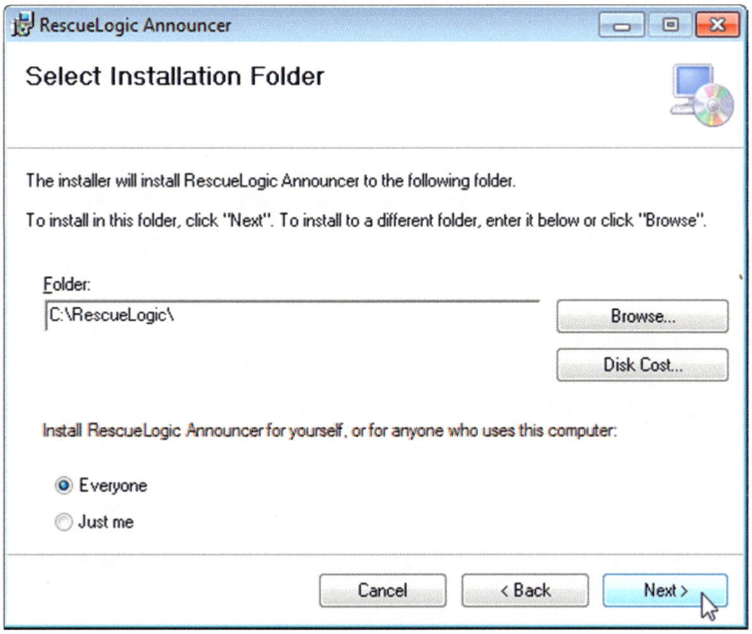

Click “Next”

Click “Next” to start the installation.

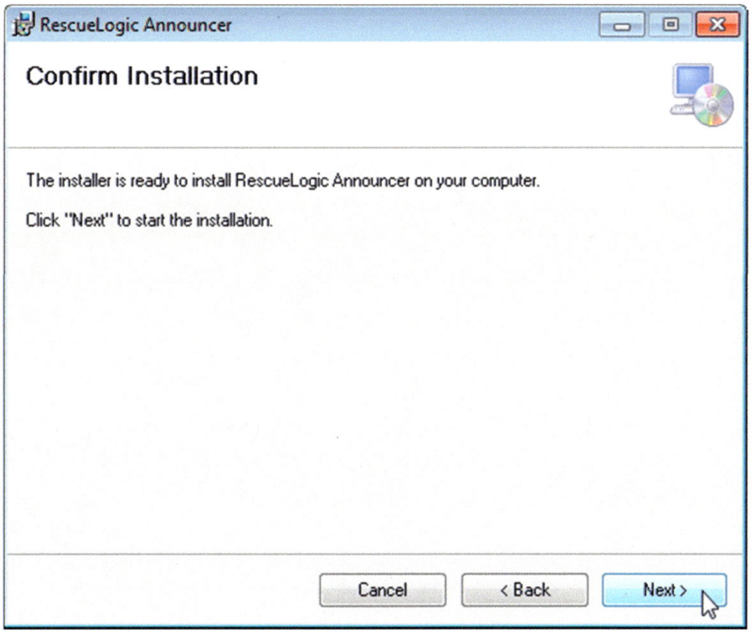

Watch the Progress Bar

You'll see the progress bar advance as installation proceeds.

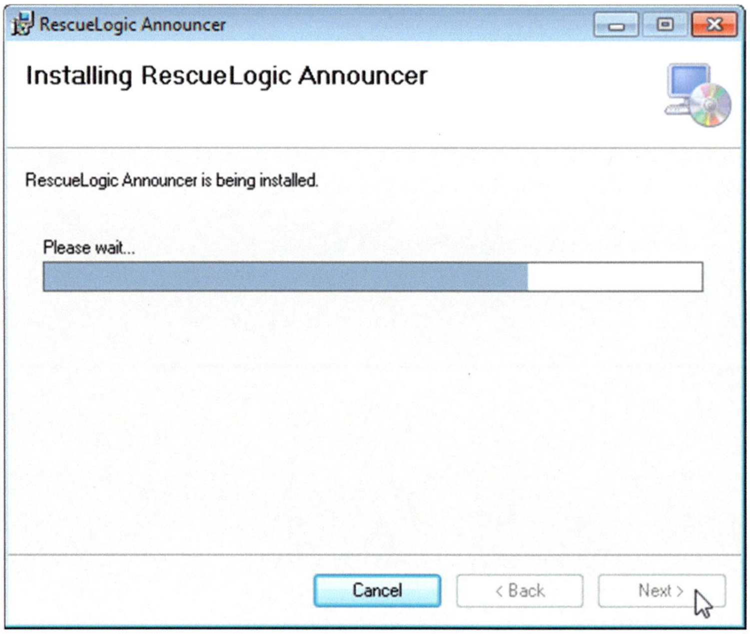

Click "Done"

Click "Done" when installation is complete.

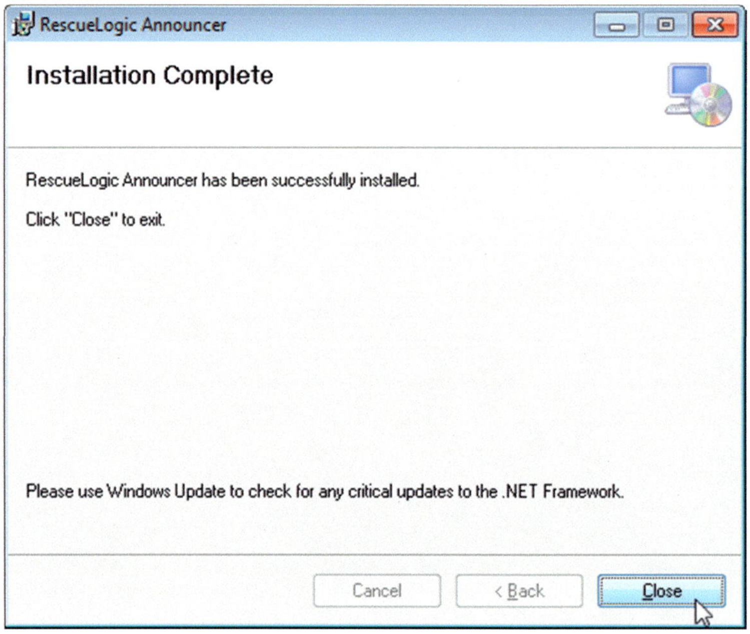

Step 2: Open the Program

To open Announcer, click on the Windows "Start" button in the lower left-hand corner of your screen. You'll see a program group called "RescueLogic," with the "Announcer" shortcut inside. Click the "Announcer" icon.

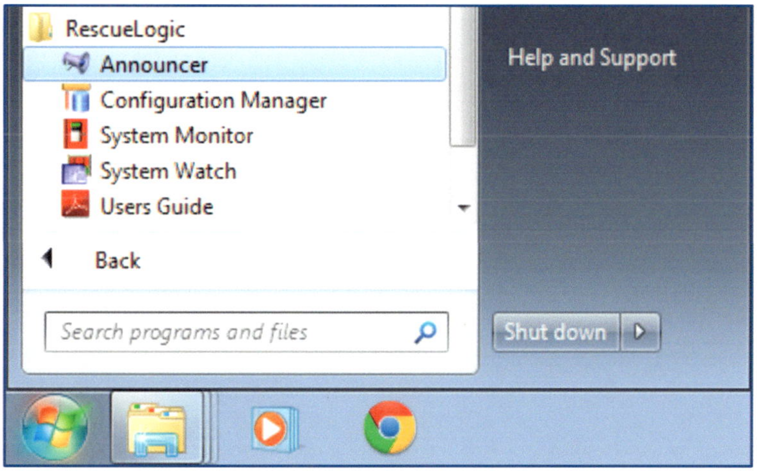

A new window will open; it logs the fact that Announcer has opened, that it found and connected to the database, and that it started polling for activity in the alarm system that's being monitored by System Monitor.

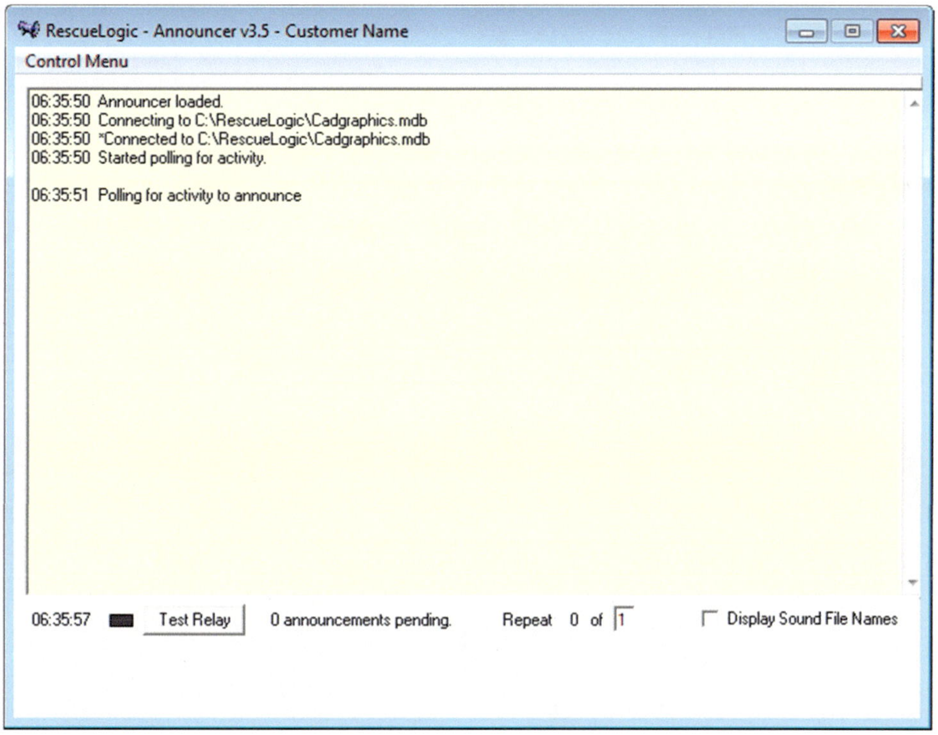

Technical Note: The same information displayed here is also being saved to a daily log file in a folder called "Announcer Logs."

Step 3: Test

Click "Control Menu" again and select "Show Test Panel." You'll see eight text boxes appear at the bottom of the Announcer information window.

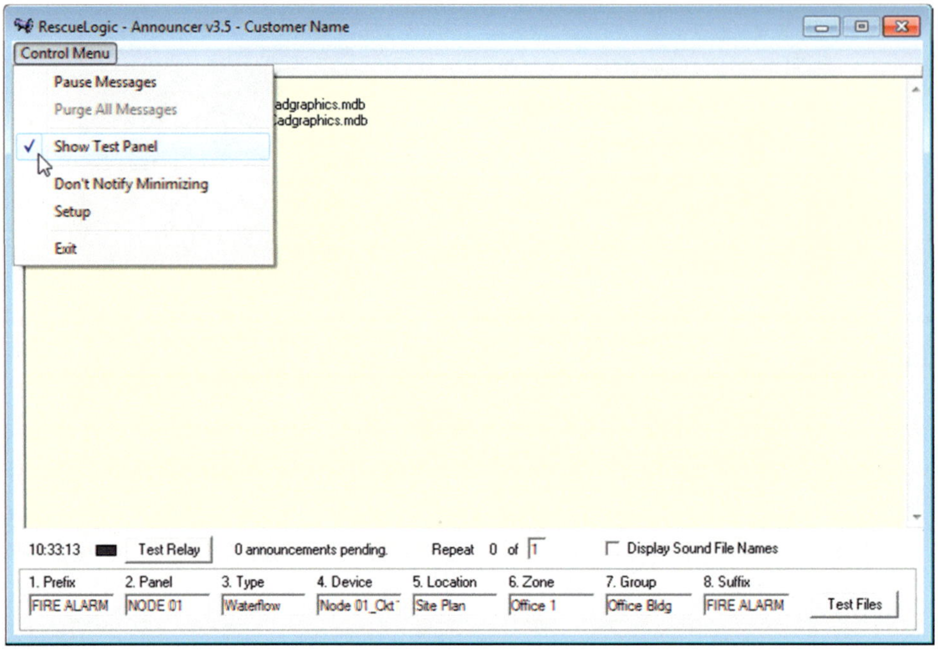

Click the checkbox that reads, "Display Sound File Names."

Announcer will look for the sound files associated with device in your system. The software comes pre-loaded with sample sound files.

In this example, the first text box is labeled "1. Prefix," and it's linked to a "FIRE ALARM.WAV" sound file.

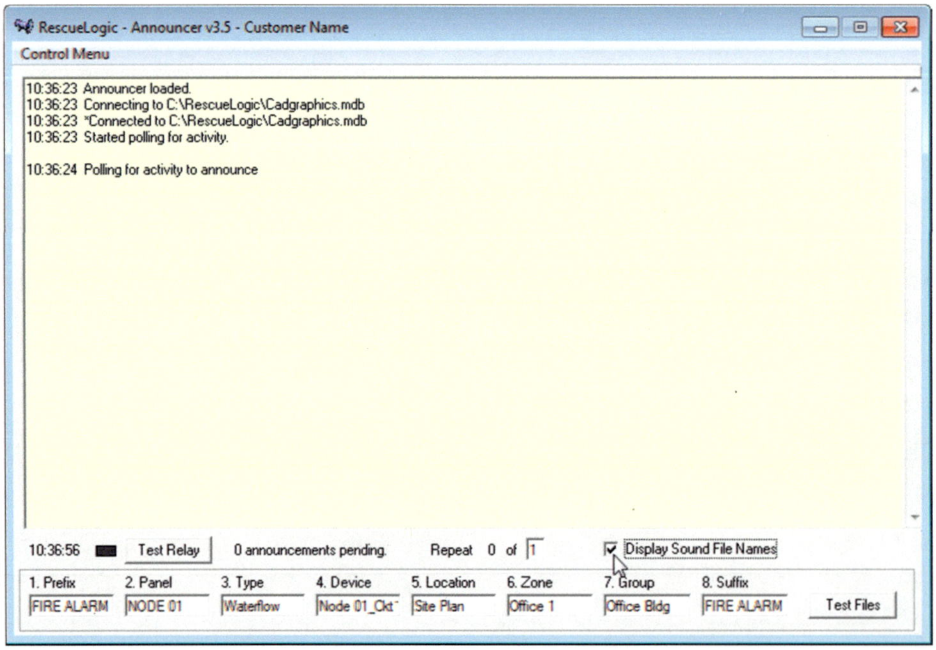

Click the "Test Files" button

Click the "Test Files" button. You will see a list of eight categories that are associated with every alarm or device in a RescueLogic system: prefix, panel, type, device, location, zone, group, and suffix.

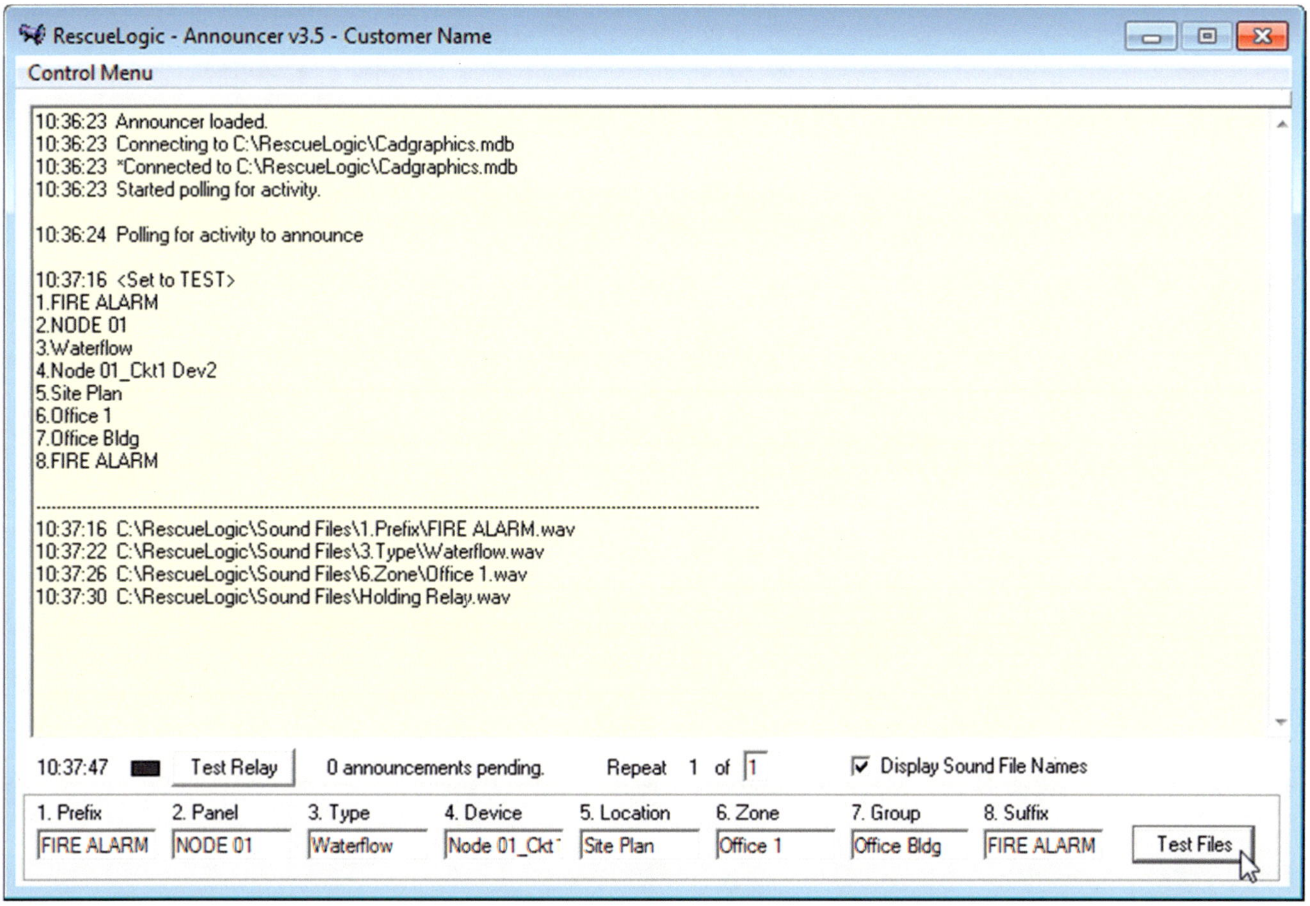

In this example, you'll notice that the Announcer program found WAV files for some of the values automatically. They're at the bottom of the list.

If your speakers are turned on, you'll hear, "Attention, attention, attention: A fire alarm is in progress." That's the prefix.

Next, you'll hear, "Sprinkler waterflow," which describes the type of device that's reporting an alarm.

Then you'll hear, "This alarm is in Office Building 1," which describes the zone.

This is how Announcer would handle a similar event in a typical system. You'll notice that Announcer uses the same data that System Watch reports; in this case, both programs are describing an alarm from a pull station.

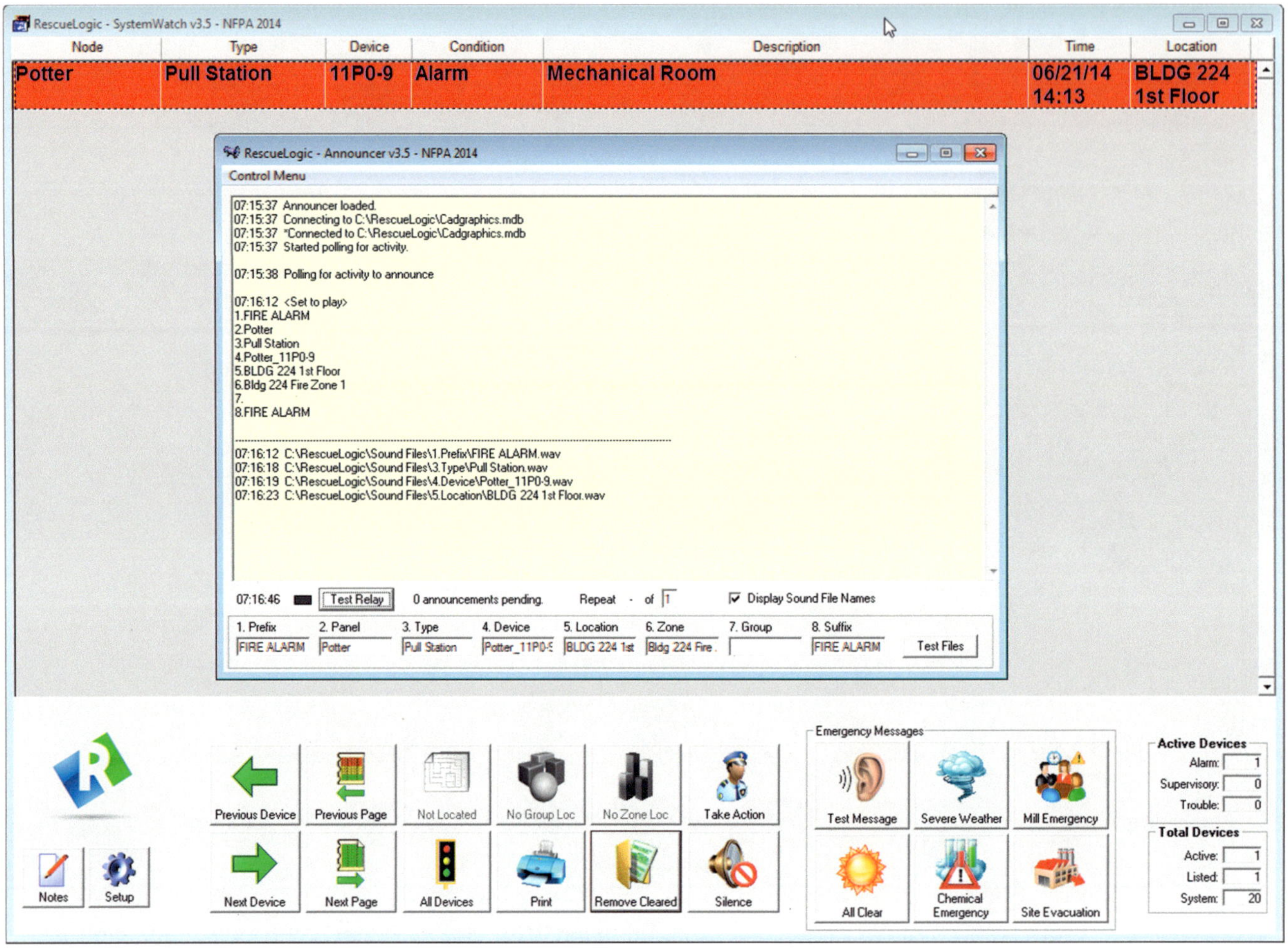

Announcer automatically locates the .WAV sound files associated with each device. In this case, Announcer found matches for the prefix, type, and location of the pull station alarm.

In the short list of items numbered 1 through 8, however, the "Group" field is empty because device 11P0-9 — a pull station — wasn't part of a group.

Likewise, the text boxes at the bottom of the Announcer window are automatically filled in when Announcer finds data that corresponds to an alarm or device.

If any of the list items or text boxes are empty after you test your system, you'll know that Announcer couldn't find a match for that category.

Helpful Hint: The sound file names for each device in your system must match their names in your RescueLogic database. You can check them by comparing each device as it's listed in the Announcer text window to the same item in the System Watch list.

Broadcast Audible Alerts about Any Device

Announcer can broadcast alerts from any device in your RescueLogic system. In this example, Announcer is sounding a supervisory alarm for a tamper switch.

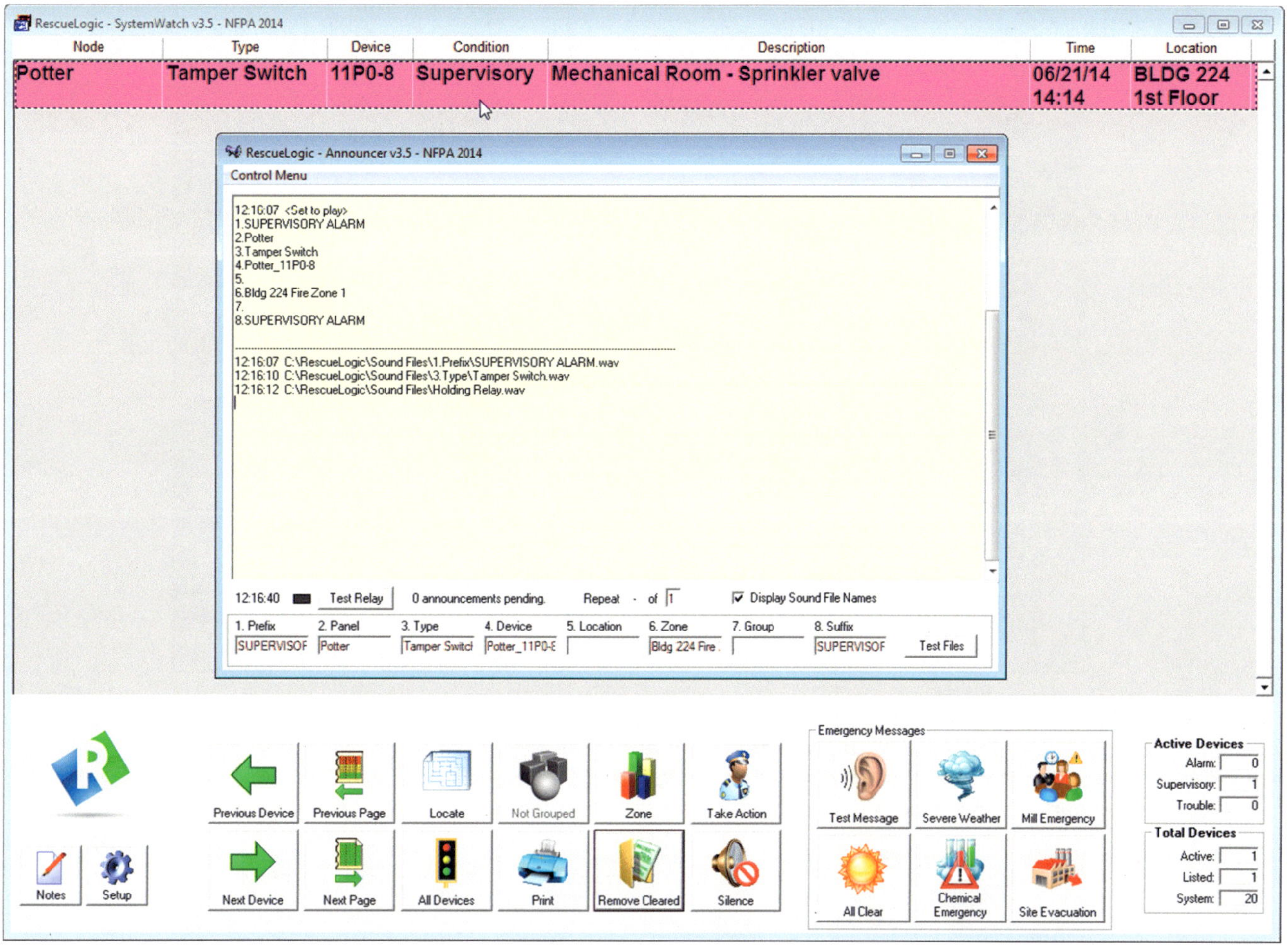

Helpful Hint: You probably won't want to broadcast every Announcer message to everyone on your site. Instead, you can set up multiple computers, and store separate sound files on each. You might want one computer at your guard station that will play fire and supervisory alarms. A second computer in the facility manager's office could play fire, supervisory, and trouble alerts. A third computer, connected to your site's public-address system, could broadcast fire alarms and emergency instructions for the general public.

An Important Note about Locating Sound Files

Announcer looks for *exact* matches between device names and associated sound files. The sound files also have to be correctly sorted into subfolders, so that Announcer can find them.

In a typical RescueLogic system, you'll have a main "Sound Files" folder, with eight subfolders that match eight categories of data for every device in your system. Each subfolder will hold sound files that correspond to individual devices.

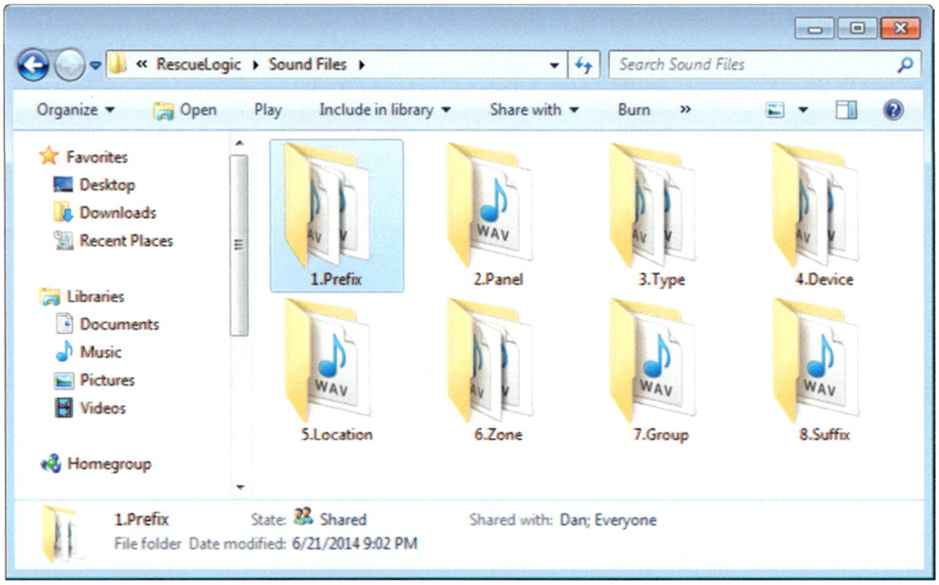

In this example, the "Prefix" folder contains a "Fire Alarm" sound file that will play for every fire alarm in your system. It will probably say something like, "Attention! Attention! Attention! A fire alarm is in progress." Likewise, the "Supervisory Alarm" sound file will play when devices report supervisory alarms like tamper switches. It will probably say something like, "Attention, please! There is a problem with the fire alarm system."

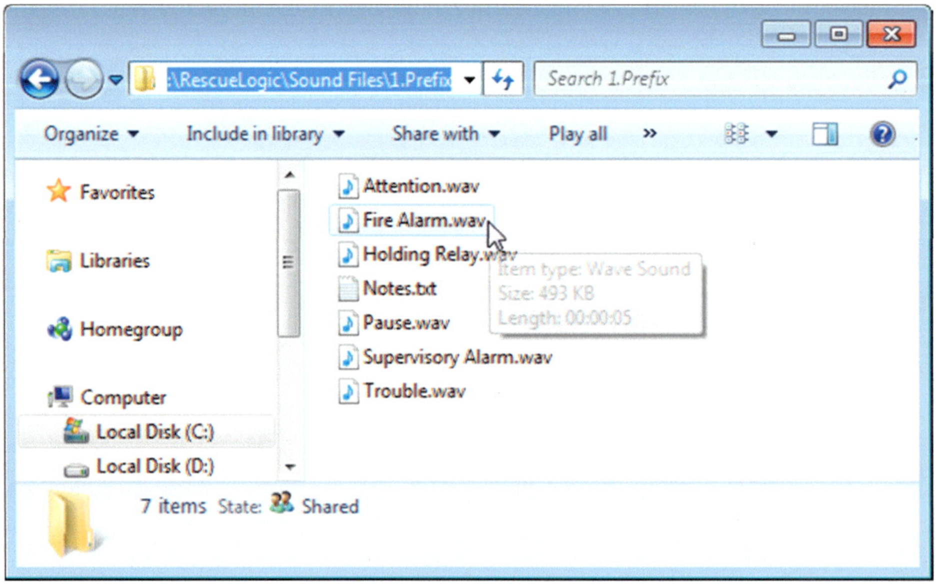

Step 4: Create Custom Sound Files for Your System

This section will show you how to create custom sound files for your Announcer system.

1. In a typical RescueLogic system, devices can report fire, supervisory, or trouble conditions. You'll start by creating three prefix messages — one for each possible condition.
2. You'll also need to create a message for every type of device in your facility, such as heat detectors, smoke detectors, and manual pull stations.
3. You'll also need to create a sound file for each location on your site, like the first, second, and third floors.
4. Optionally, you can also create message segments for zones and groups of devices, as well as individual devices and panels.

Convert Text to Speech

If you haven't done so yet, download and install the professional version of the NaturalReader text-to-speech program, available from www.naturalreaders.com.

Open the program and hit "Play" to hear the welcome message aloud.

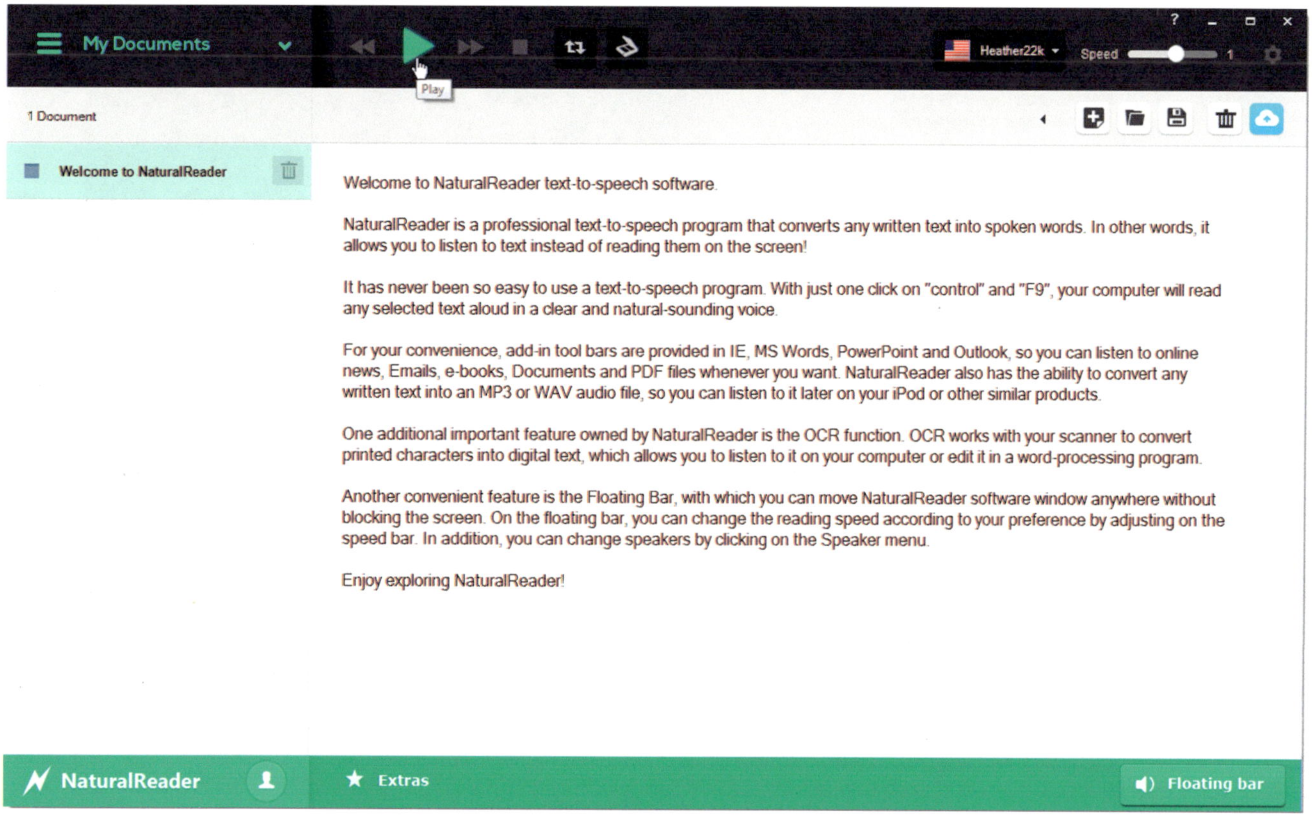

Click the floating bar in the lower-right corner, and a floating control panel will open.

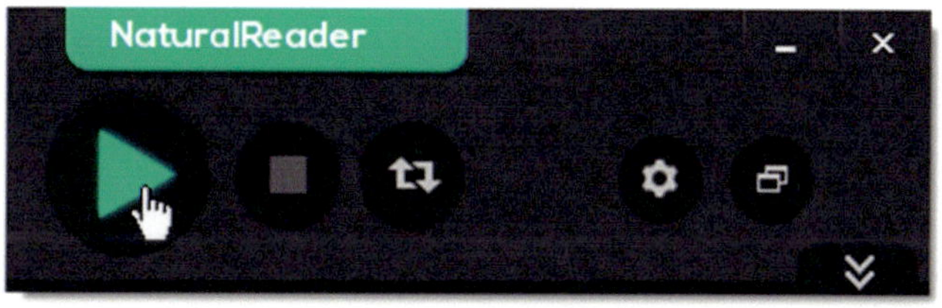

The "Alarm Sounds" Text File

Look in your Announcer program folder for the "Alarm Sounds" text file. Open it; you can use the samples in the list as a starting point for your own sound files.

Highlight a line of text, as shown, and click the "Play" arrow on the NaturalReader control panel. You'll hear the text aloud.

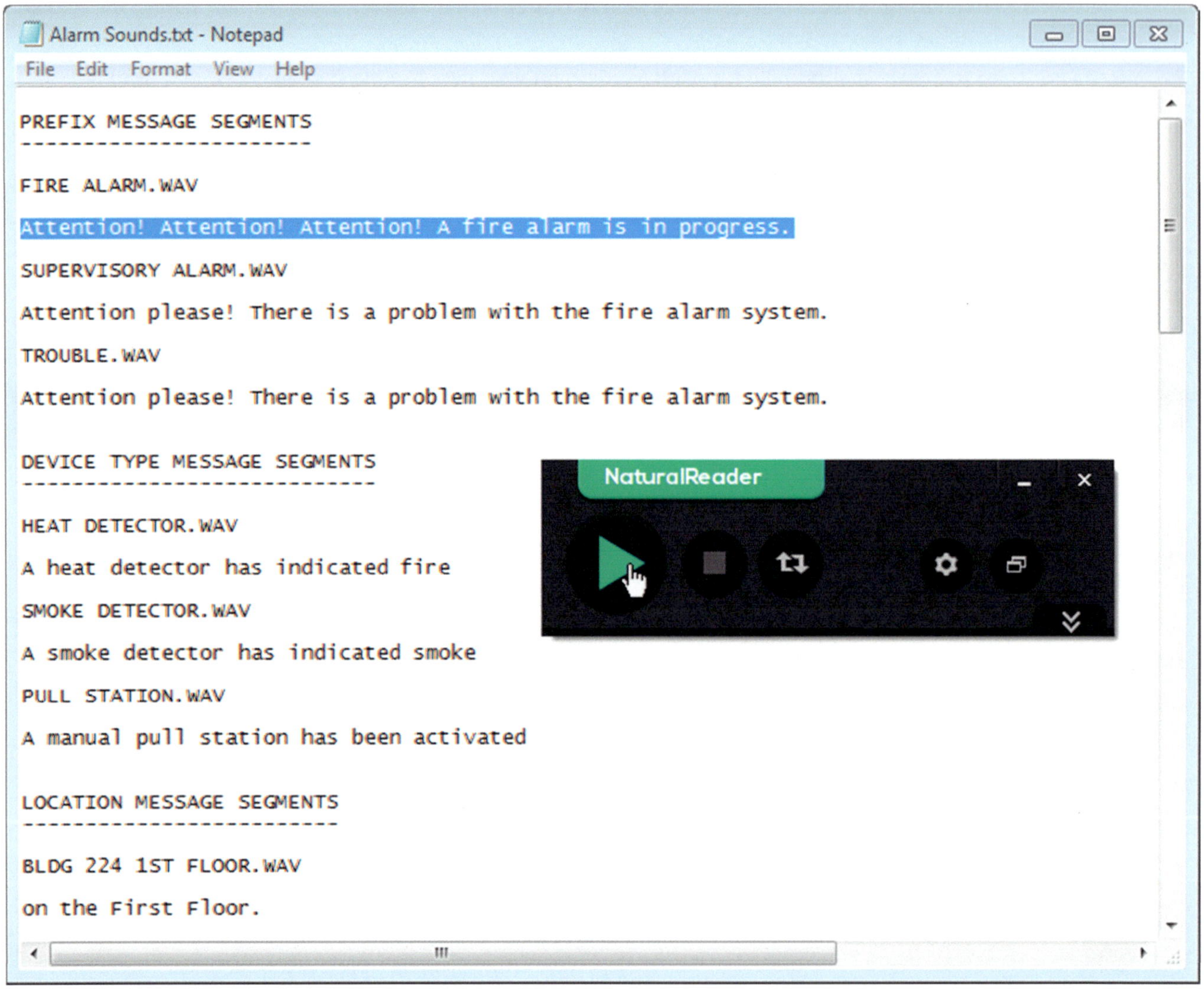

Helpful Hint: Look carefully at the text file, and you'll see how the Announcer program will mix and match message segments for various emergencies.

You might hear an alert that says, "Attention! Attention! Attention! A fire alarm is in progress. A heat detector has indicated fire on the First Floor."

Alternately, the message segments in the illustration might also broadcast an emergency alert that says, "Attention please! There is a problem with the fire alarm system. A smoke detector has indicated smoke on the First Floor."

Convert Text to Speech

Click the “Convert” button to convert the highlighted text you selected into a sound file.

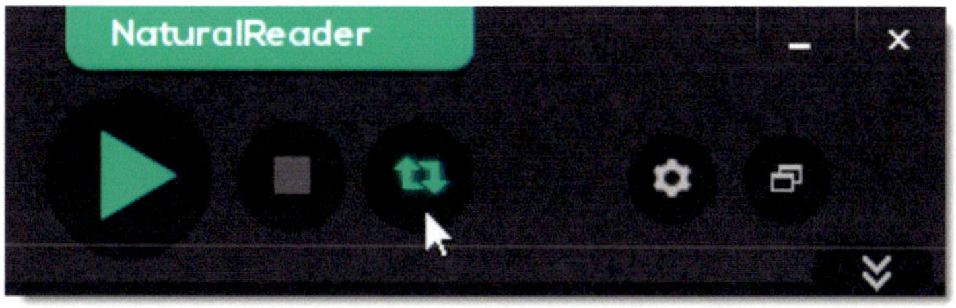

Choose the WAV format.

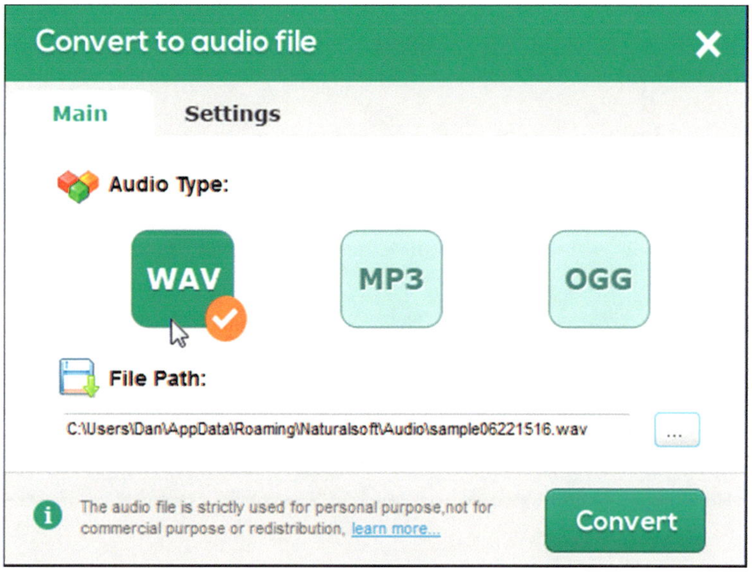

Browse to save the file to the correct RescueLogic subfolder.

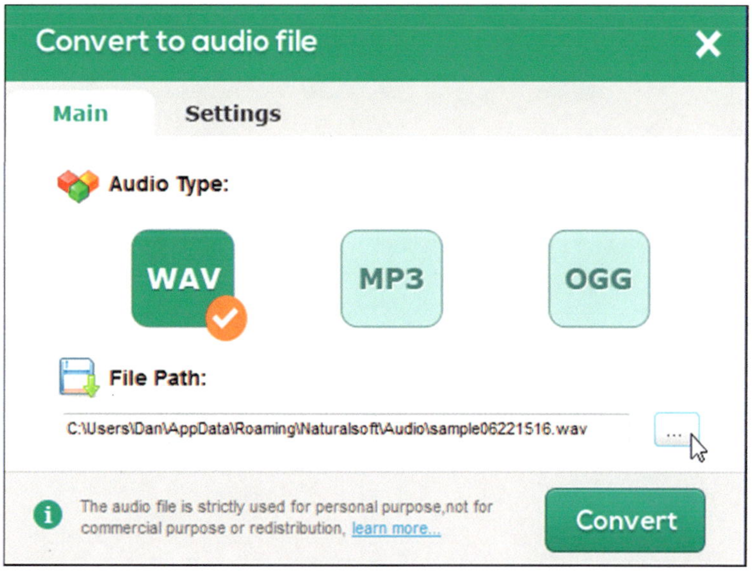

Save the Sound Files

Make sure you save prefix messages in the "Prefix" subfolder.

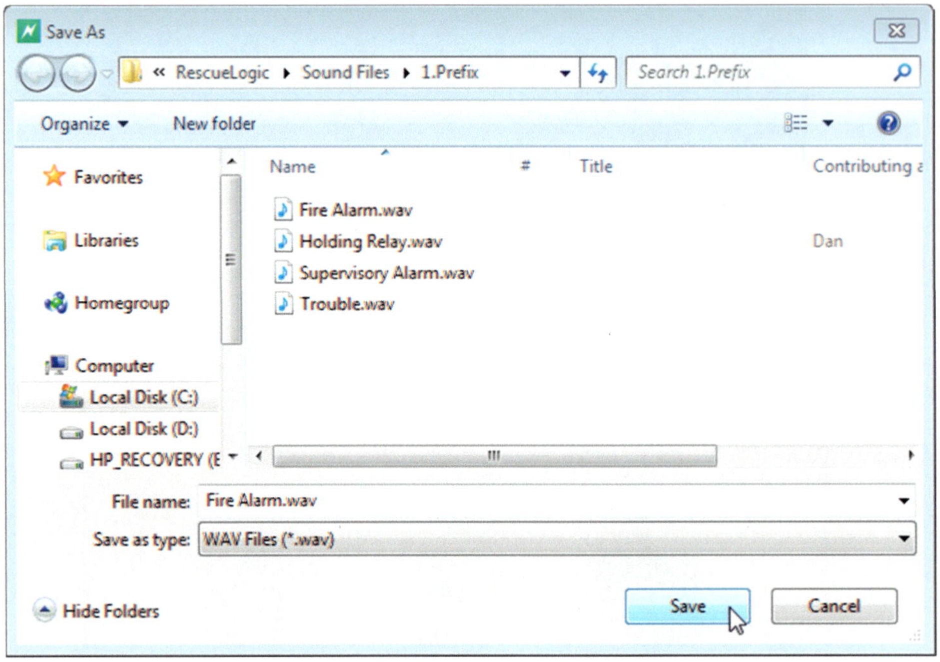

Click "Convert."

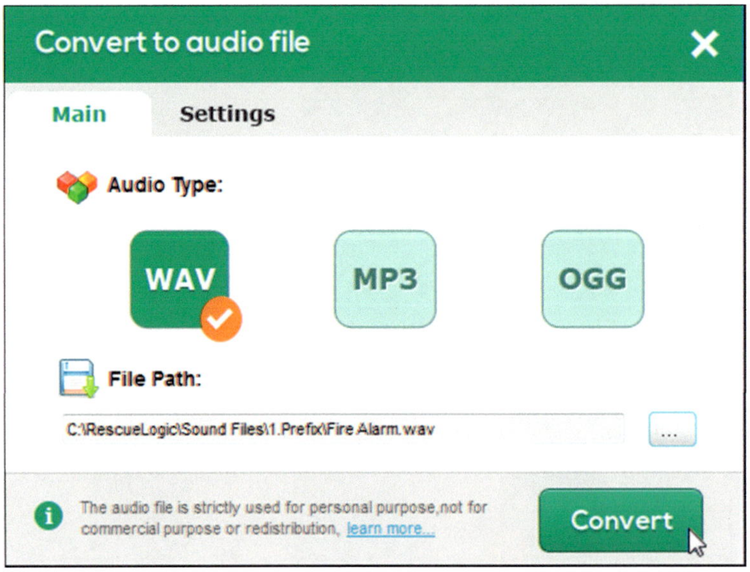

Test Your Sound File

You'll see that your sound file has been created.

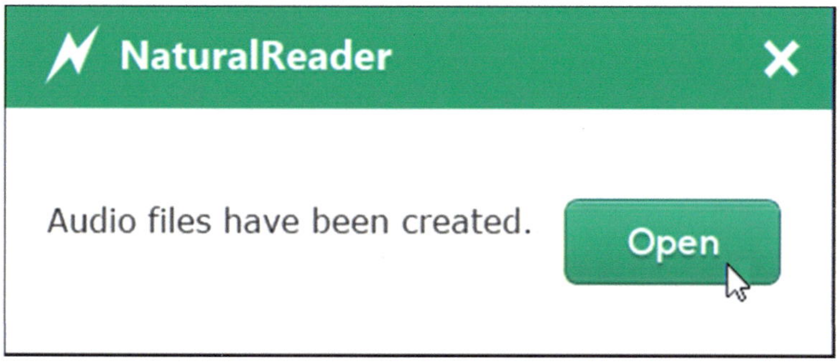

A new window will open so you can test your new sound file.

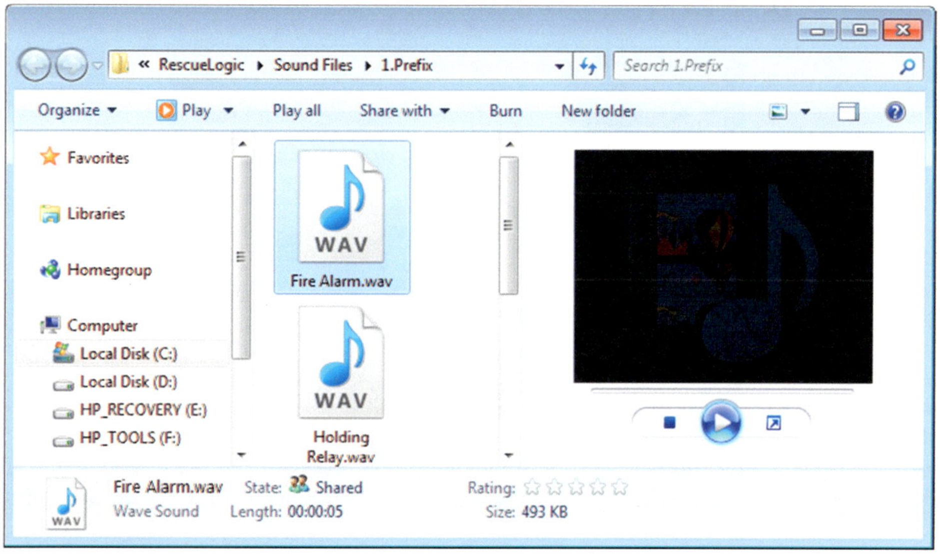

Make More Sound Files

Repeat the same steps to create sound files for fire, supervisory, or trouble conditions.

Create a message for every type of device in your facility, such as heat detectors, smoke detectors, and manual pull stations.

You'll also need to create a sound file for each location on your site, like the first, second, and third floors.

Optionally, you can also create message segments for zones and groups of devices, as well as individual devices and panels.

As you proceed, make sure the names of your sound files match the names in your database, and be sure to save the sound files in the correct subfolders.

Test Your Work

Test your work by running all three RescueLogic programs at once: System Monitor, System Watch, and Announcer. If necessary, click the Windows "Start" button in the lower left-hand corner of your screen. You'll see a program group called "RescueLogic." Click on the programs to open them.

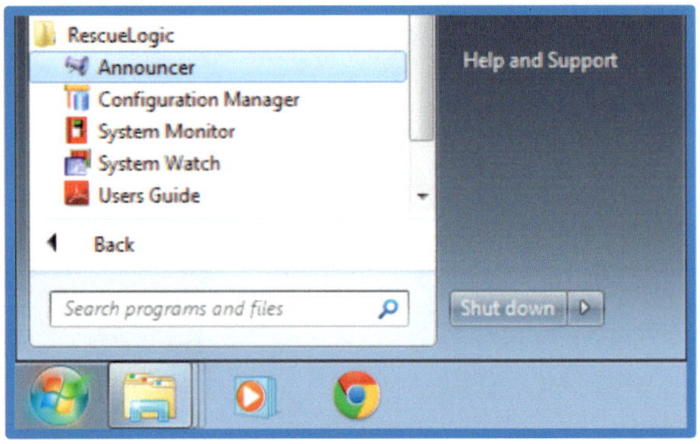

Have one of your technicians walk through your site and trigger a representative sample of the alarms in your system. If you don't hear audible alerts from the Announcer program, check your sound file names and locations.

Step 5: Connect to Your Public Address System

If you plan to connect your RescueLogic system to a public address system, you'll need an ADAM-6060 relay module, available online or from industrial control suppliers.

The ADAM module will relay emergency messages, but it will keep your computer's other sounds — like the Windows startup chime — from being broadcast over your public address system.

You'll connect the ADAM module to your Ethernet network, and RescueLogic will find it via its IP address. To start the configuration process, click on the Control Menu and choose "Setup."

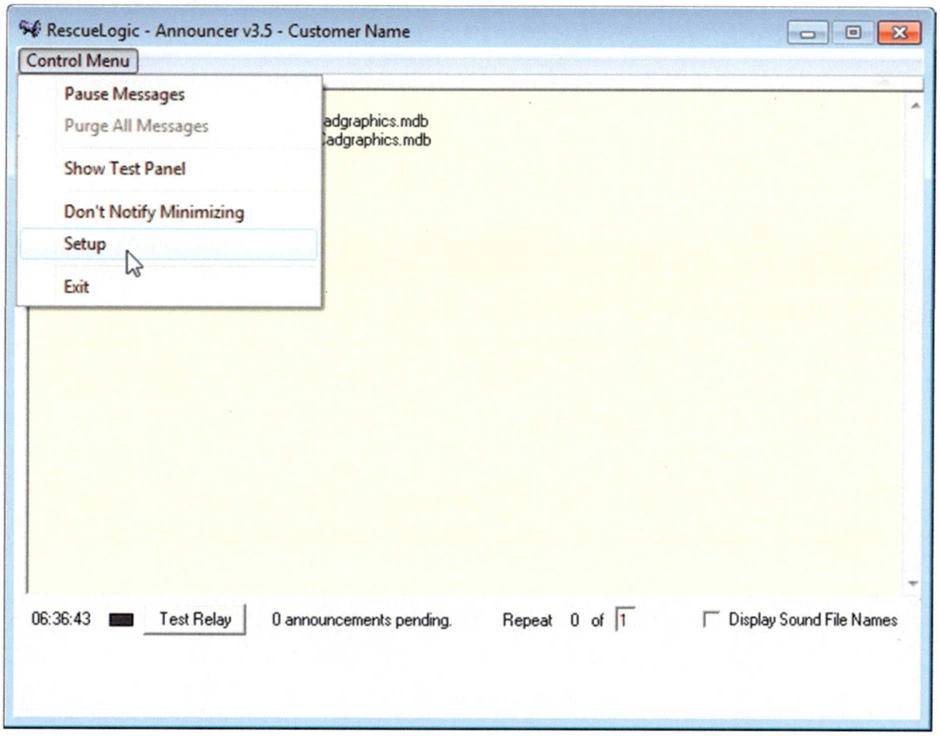

Enter the IP Address

A new window will open, with settings for an optional control relay. Enter the ADAM module's IP address. Leave the timeouts set to the default.

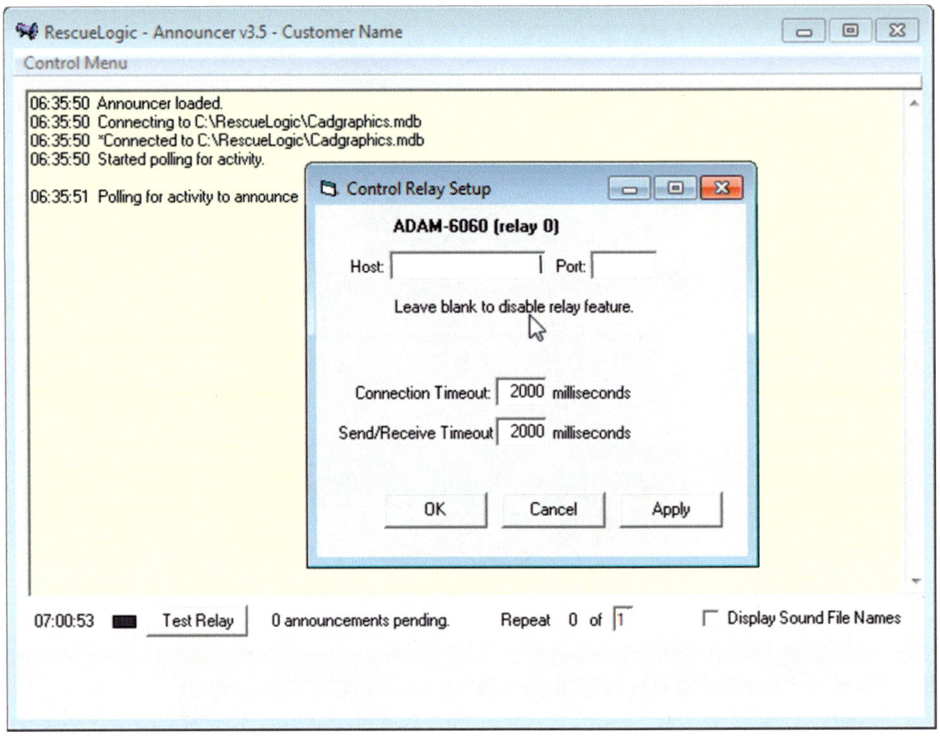

Click "Apply" and "OK."

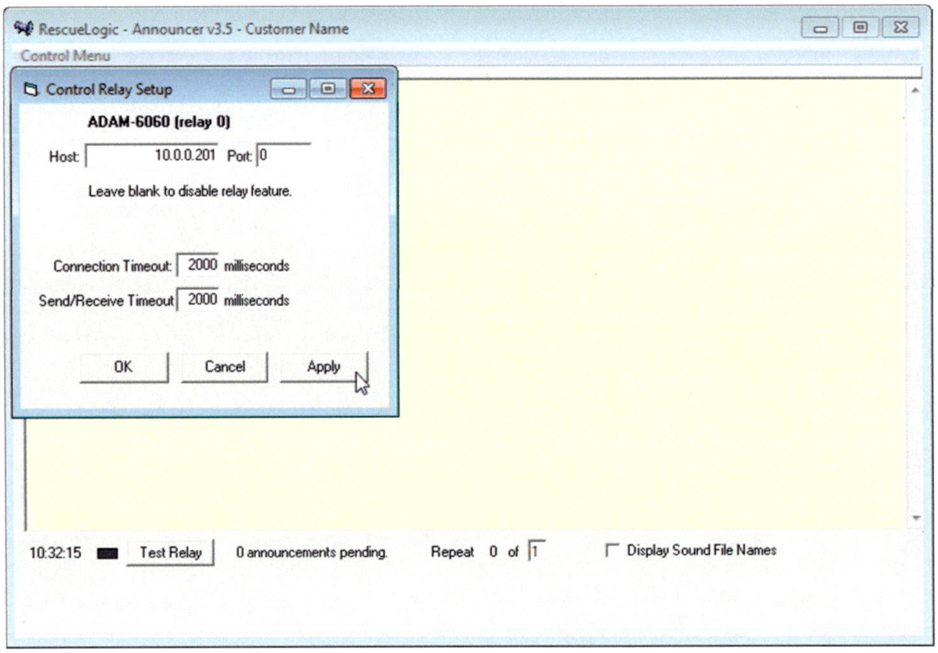

Check the Connection

You'll see the primary Announcer window again. Click the "Test Relay" button. This screen shows what you'll see if the Ethernet cable isn't connected to the ADAM module.

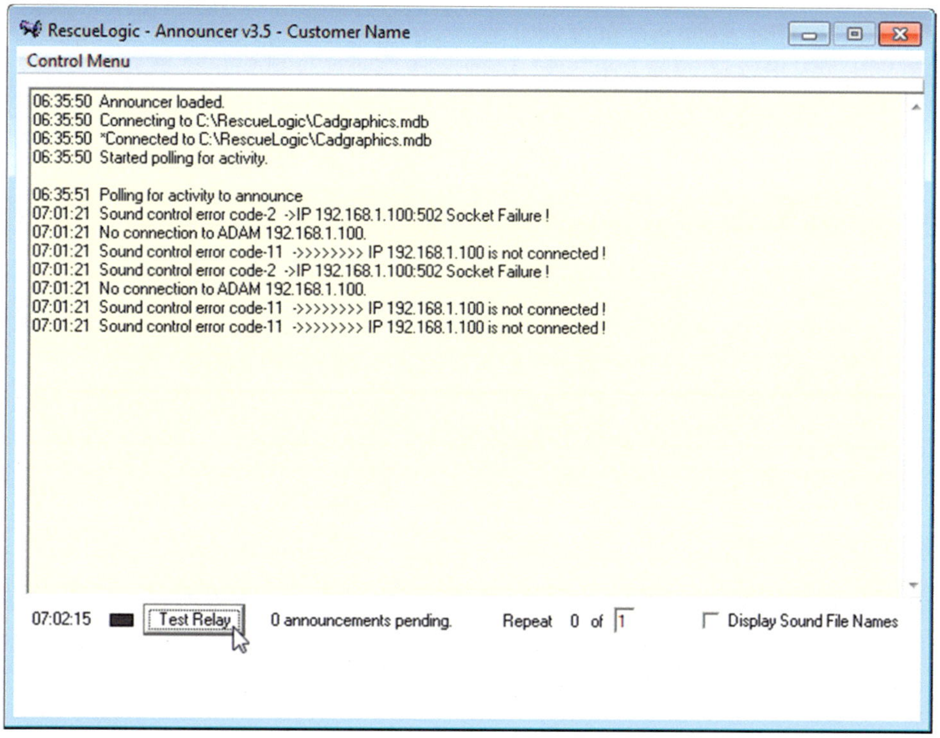

If you click test and the indicator light turns green, you'll hear a clicking sound from the ADAM module relay. That means the relay is ready to allow audible messages to be broadcast over your public-address system; the light will turn green whenever the relay is turned on.

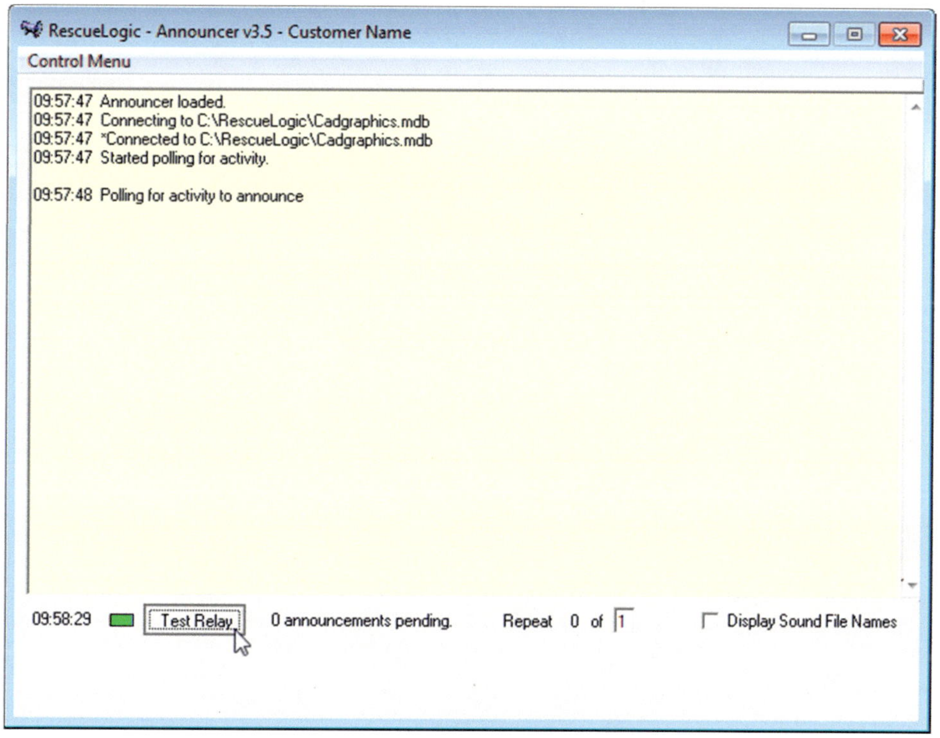

Connect Your Computer to the ADAM Module

Use one audio cable to connect the speaker jack on your computer to the ADAM module, and a second audio cable to connect the ADAM module to the input jack on your public address system. Follow the manufacturer's instructions or consult your installer if you need help with those connections.

You will need to ensure that the audio output of your computer has enough power to be compatible with your public address system. You may need to purchase a pre-amp device to boost the signal.

Step 7: Request Custom Messages

The Announcer program generates most of its emergency messages by combining information about device types, status, and location. We can also create custom "canned" messages specifically for your site.

Custom messages come with their own push-button controls, and appear at the bottom of the System Watch screen. Guards, dispatchers, and first responders can use the buttons to broadcast emergency messages over a public-address system.

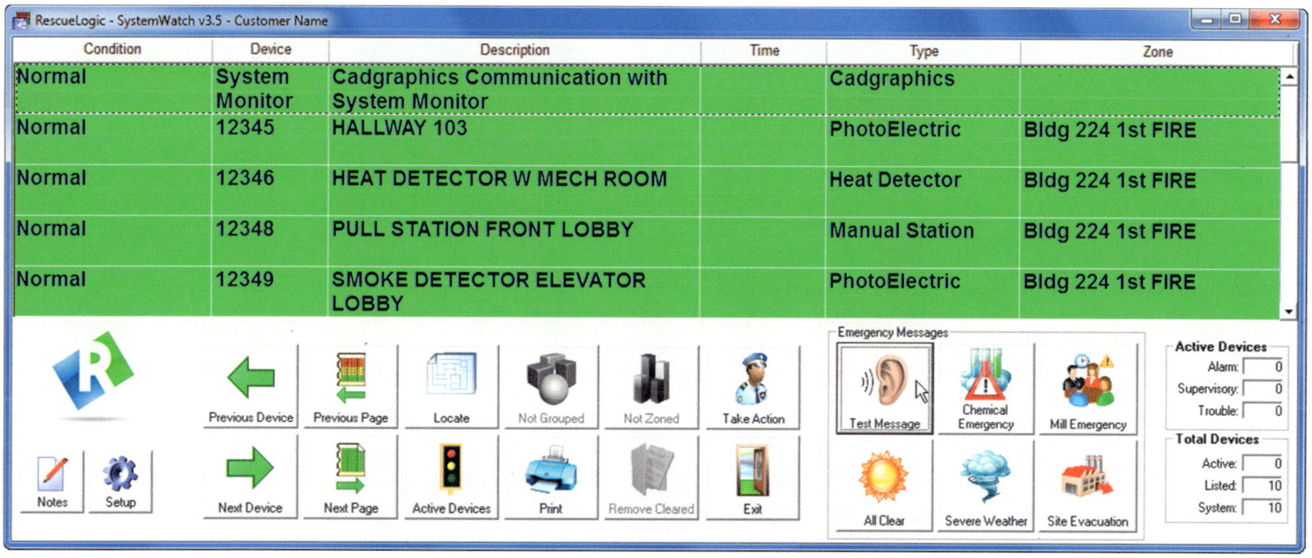

This screen shows emergency messages that were customized for a paper mill. They include a:

- Test message. A system administrator will use this button during on-site tests and emergency drills, with an audible announcement that says, "This is a test. This is only a test."
- Chemical emergency warning, typically used for chemical spills, hazardous material events.
- Mill emergency alert, which could sound a "shelter in place" message.
- Severe weather announcement, to broadcast storm and tornado warnings.
- Site evacuation command, which would order everyone to leave the premises.
- And an "all clear," to let everyone know that an emergency situation has ended, so it's safe to go about their normal business.

To request custom messaging for your site, call us at (612) 722-3233.

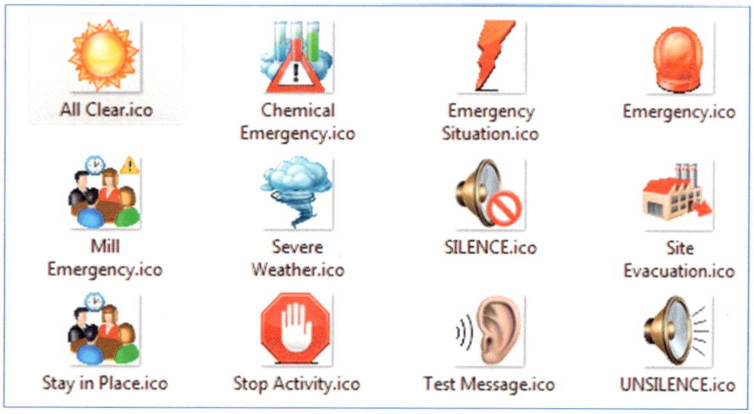

Step 8: Keep Announcer Running

The Announcer program won't work if it's been turned off, or if System Monitor has been turned off.

If Announcer isn't running, turn it on. Just click on the Windows "Start" button in the lower left-hand corner of your screen. You'll see a program group called "RescueLogic." Open the program group and click "Announcer." You can follow the same procedure to start System Monitor, too.

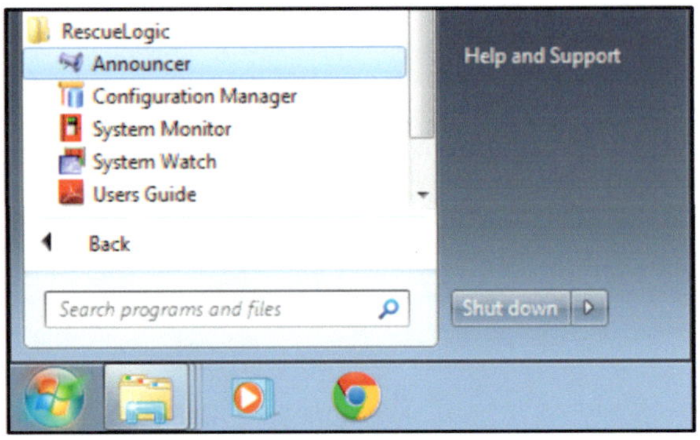

If the programs are running, but minimized, you can see their icons in the lower right corner of the screen.

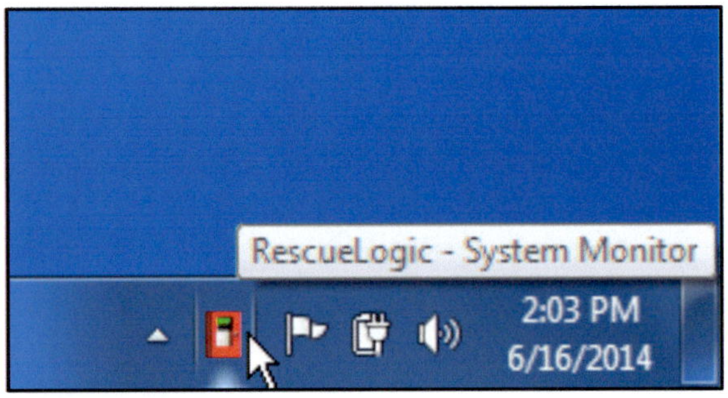

If you can't see them, check the hidden icons.

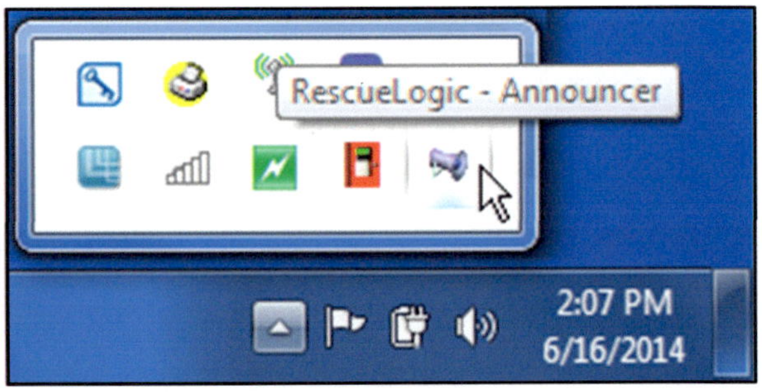

Questions or Comments?

Technical support is available online at RescueLogic.com, or by phone at (612) 722-3233.

Copyright Information

ISBN

ISBN 978-0692244296.

Ordering Information

You can order professionally printed copies of this guide from Amazon.com. Overnight delivery is available.

Patent Information

This guide contains proprietary information. Cadgraphics and RescueLogic techniques and technology are protected by United States Patents 6,229,429 and 6,369,695.

Trademark Information

Cadgraphics and RescueLogic are registered trademarks of Cadgraphics Incorporated. “Safety Made Simple” is the service mark of Cadgraphics Incorporated. Other products mentioned herein are used for identification purposes only and may be trademarks or service marks of their respective companies. All terms mentioned in this book that are known to be trademarks or service marks have been appropriately capitalized. Cadgraphics Incorporated cannot attest to the accuracy of this information. The use of a term in this guide should not be regarded as affecting the validity of any trademark or service mark.

Disclaimer

Although every precaution has been taken in the preparation of this guide, the author and the publisher assume no responsibility for errors or omissions. The information in this guide is subject to change without notice to improve reliability, design, and function. This guide does not represent a commitment or a contract on behalf of Cadgraphics Incorporated. In no event will Cadgraphics Incorporated, its agents, or its representatives be liable for direct, indirect, special, incidental, or consequential damages arising out of the use or inability to use the product or documentation, even if advised of the possibility of such damages. The entire risk as to the results and performance of Cadgraphics RescueLogic software is assumed by you.